Aruz classical poetics
Teaching and methodical guide

Ismailov Is'haqjon Otabayevich

Bobonazarova, Gulzoda Alishervich

©Ismailov Is'hoqjon Otaboyevich
Aruz classical poetics - Teaching and methodical guide
by: Ismailov Is'hoqjon Otaboyevich
Bobonazarova Gulzoda
Edition: July '2024
Publisher:
Taemeer Publications LLC (Michigan, USA / Hyderabad, India)

ISBN 978-93-5872-427-1

9 789358 724271

© Ismailov Is'hoqjon Otaboyevich

Book	:	Aruz classical poetics — Teaching and methodical guide
Author	:	Ismailov Is'hoqjon Otaboyevich Bobonazarova Gulzoda
Publisher	:	Taemeer Publications
Year	:	'2024
Pages	:	114
Title Design	:	*Taemeer Web Design*

RESPONSIBLE EDITOR:

San'atbek SARIYEV, Doctor of Philological Sciences, Associate Professor

REVIEWERS:

Bekposhsha RAHIMOVA
Philological Sciences doctor, associate professor

Nasiba SOBIROVA, doctor of philology, associate professor

Mumtoz poetics is based on three sciences. These are: ilmi aruz, ilmi badi' and ilmi kafiya. In the history of our literature, these three sciences together have been considered the criterion for determining the elegance of classical poetry and the poet's potential. Among them, the science of aruz is considered relatively complex, and not knowing it well makes it difficult to understand the essence of artistic examples created in classical genres.

In this sense, "Introduction to Aruz and Classical Poetics" is a clear and important study of Aruz weight and its rules, ways of determining the size of works written in Aruz, the place of Aruz system in Uzbek classical literature, classical genres and their art, science of art and science of rhyme. serves as a determining basis for conveying information to the student. Therefore, this subject is of particular importance in the establishment of Uzbek language and literature education in higher educational institutions. Complete mastery of the subject "Introduction to Aruz and Classical Poetics" prepares the ground for strengthening the knowledge of undergraduate students, developing artistic taste and literary perception, and forming research skills in them. In this process, careful preparation for control questions becomes important in the further formation of students' skills.

It was recommended for publication at the meeting of the Methodological Council of Urganch State University on June 20, 2024. (Report No. 11)

Short Question Papers.

TICKET #1

1. Determine the weight of the following byte of Babur
   If he comes, I won't be disloyal,
   if I turn my face, I won't be. – – V / – V – V / V – – V / – V – (**Muzore'i musmali akhrabi makfufi mahzuf**)

2. Determine the weight of the following verse of Babur.

   I'm so happy, I'm so happy, I'm so happy,
   I'm so happy. B – B – / VV – – / B – B – / – – (**Praise the beloved of Mujtassi**)

3. What is the name of a ghazal with an internal rhyme? - **Ghazali musajja'**

4. What is the name of a poem with nine verses in each stanza? – **Mutass'a**

5. What is the name of a poem written in two

languages in a certain order? - Shiru-shakar

6. What is the name of the farm of Hazaj Bay? - **maqbuz**

7. Each volume is equal to a ghazal and is a poem made up of stanzas that rhyme like a ghazal, in which the two verses at the end of each stanza have independent melodiousness. What lyrical genre are we talking about? – **Tarkibband**

8. What is the result of the repetition of foilotun and mustafilun? - **Khafif**

9. What is the name of the poem, which was formed directly in Turkish literature, is written in the musad of strict ramali in maqsur weight, consists of four lines, and at the end of the line, radifs consist of homonymous words? - **Tuyuq**

10. What is the name of the change of the Ramal Sea (VV - -)? – **Makhbun**

11. What is the name of Mustafilun's main residence? - **mahbun**

12. Who first used the term "poetics"? - **Aristotle**

13. It is one of the spiritual arts and at the same time a poetic genre. In this case, the poem is

mainly written in the form of a ghazal, and the name of a person or thing comes from the combination of letters at the beginning of the verses of the poem. What is it about here? - **Muvashshah**

14. What is the result of the repetition of Mustaf'ilun, Mustaf'ilun, Ma'f'alotu? -**Sari'**

15. What is the result of the repetition of mafaiylun, failotun? - **Muzori'**

16. What is the name of a riddle-poem that consists of one stanza, sometimes two-three stanzas, written on the basis of an emphasis or hint, which relies on hiding something through Arabic letters? – **Problem**

17. What is the name of a poem with seven verses in each stanza? - **Musabba'**.

18. Mustafilun, what is the result of repeating an activity? – **Mujtass**

19. Which bahr is formed from the repetition of Mafailatun verse? – **Wafir**

20. What is the name of the art of referring to famous historical events, legends, literary works

or proverbs in poetry or prose? - **Talmih**

21. What is the name of the four-line poem on romantic, moral, political-philosophical topics, which is widely used in Uzbek classical literature, written in the Akhram and Akhrab genealogies of Hazaj Bahr? - **Ruba'i**

22. Mustaf'ilun, what is the result of repetition of maf'alotu? - **Munsarih**

23. What is the name of the art of providing a poetic reason for an event described in literary works? - **husni talil**

24. What is the name of the art based on giving an example of a life event in the second verse as evidence for the idea expressed in the first verse of the poem? - **Tamsil**

25. What is the name of the art of quoting a folk proverb to prove a point expressed in poetry and prose? - **Irsoli parable**

TICKET #2

1. Determine the weight of Alisher Navoi below
   Look at my eyes, come and do science,
   make a country like a people under my eyes. B – B – / VV – – / B – B – / – –
   (Mujtassi musamli mahbuni maktu')

2. Determine the weight of the following verse of Babur.
   Hajj of the month of Ghurbat made me old,
   Hijran and Ghurbat affected me. – – V / V – – V / V – – V / V – ~ (**Hazaji musmali akhrabi makfufi maqsur**)

3. What is the name of a lyrical poem that expresses grief in connection with the death of someone? - **Marcia**

4. This art refers to sequentially mentioning the names of several things or concepts in a verse, and then sequentially stating judgments about them. What kind of art are you talking about? - **Laff and publication**

5. What is the name of a riddle-poem that consists of one stanza, sometimes two-three stanzas,

written on the basis of an emphasis or hint, which relies on hiding something through Arabic letters? - **Problem**

6. What is the name of the art of referring to famous historical events, legends, literary works or proverbs in poetry or prose? – **Talmih**

7. What is the name of a poem with seven verses in each stanza? - **Musabba'**.

8. What is the name of the art of using a word in a literary work in a different sense than its own meaning, expressing the meaning of "taking something for a deposit (temporarily)", or rather, not in its real sense, but in a figurative sense? ? – **Metaphor**

9. What is the result of repetition of Mafailatun verse? - **Wafir**

10. Mustafilun, what is the result of repetition of activities? – **Mujtass**

11. It is an ornate couplet, and the poem has not one, but two rhymes. What kind of rhyme is it about? – **Zulqafiyatain**

12. If all the words in two verses rhyme with each

other, what type of rhyme is considered? - **tarsi'**

13. Life is hard for someone, and death is death when you open it to someone. What is the name of using opposite words as a rhyme? - **Contrast rhyme**

14. What is the general name of the series of poetic forms widely used in Eastern classical poetry, which means "to string pearls on a string", "to arrange" in Arabic? – **Musammat**

15. What is the name of a poem written in two languages in a certain order? -**Shiru-shakar**

16. What is the name of the mafaoilun afoyil of the Hazaj Sea? **Maqbuz**

17 What poetic art did the poet use in the stanza? - **ratio**

18. What is the result of the repetition of foilotun and mustafilun? - **Light**

19. What is the name of a rhyme that occurs in more than two rhyme styles, but the lines do not rhyme completely? - **Zulqavafi'**

20. What is the name of the smallest one-stanza poem in classical literature? - **Fard**

21. What is the rhyming type of rubai in the order a+a+a+a usually called? - **taronai ruboiy**

22. What is the name of the lyrical genre in a solemn style that praises famous historical figures and great events? - **Ode**

23. Who is the author of the philosophical ode "Tuhfatul Afkor" ("Gift of Thoughts")? - **A. Navoi**

24. What is the name of the art of exaggerating and intensifying the state or movement of an artistic symbol depicted in a literary work, which means "enlargement", "strengthening" in Arabic? – **Exaggeration**

25. What is the name of fa'lun (– –) of the root of foilotun? – **praise**

TICKET #3

1–question. Determine the following weight of Alisher Navoi.

Wake up your two beautiful girls from their sweet sleep,

Play in the flower garden until they fall asleep. – – V / V – – – / – – V / V – – – (**Khazaji musmali akhrab**)

2. Determine the weight of the following ghazali of Alisher Navoi.

Soda sheikh forbids me to love you, Dema soda sheikh,

I say loda sheikh. B – – /B – – / B – – / B ~ (**Mutaqaribi musmali maqsur**)

3. What is the name of the fa' (–) zihof of the original Mafoiylun? – **Abtar**

4. What is the name of the muftailun (– VV –) of Mustafilun asli? –**matviy**

5. What is the name of the root of foiloton (VV - ~)? – **mahbuni musabbag'**

6. What is the name of fa'lun (– –) zihof of the original fauvlun? - **aslam**

7. Determine the weight of Ogahi's ghazal, which begins with "Mushkin's brow..."

   - How dare Ogahi open his mouth and say a word,

   the attack of a hundred sad deeds is difficult and unpleasant. – – V – / – – V – / – – V – / – – V – **RAJAZI MUSAMMANI SOLIM**

8. What is the name of the mafoiylu (V – – V) zihof of Mafoiylun asli? - **makfuf** 9. In what type of poem, the same text is produced even if you read it sideways and from top to bottom? - **musoviyat-tarafayn**

10. What is the name of a poem written in two languages in a certain order? -**Shiru-shakar**

11. What is the name of the shelter of the sea of Hazaj? – **maqbuz**

12. One of the tools of artistic representation widely used in our classical literature, whose root is the Arabic word "person", is given correctly in which answer? - **diagnosis**

13. Which result is formed from the repetition of foilotun and mustafilun? - **Light**

14. What is the name of a rhyme that occurs in more than two rhyme styles, but the lines do not rhyme completely? - **Zulqawafi'**

15. What is the name of the rhyming type of rubai in the order a+a+a+a, usually? - **taronai ruboiy**

16. What is the name of the lyrical genre in a solemn style that praises famous historical figures and great events? – **Ode**

17. Who is the author of the philosophical ode "Tuhfatul Afkor" ("Gift of Thoughts")? - **A.Navoiy**

18. What is the literary genre that describes the spiritual experience and emotions that are pictures of the inner world of a person? - **Lyrical type**

19. In which sea were the works of Amir Khusrav "Oinai Iskandari" and Jami's "Khiradnomai Iskandari" created? – **Subjunctive mahzuf (B – –/ B – – / B – – / B –)**

20. Which juzv does the pattern (VV –) belong

to? - **Fosilayi sugro**

21. In which poetic art can elements such as means and basis be found? - **tashbih** 22. In which season was Navoi's "Sabbayi Sayor" created? – **Khafif**

23. Which word is formed from the repetition of foilotun, mustafilun? – **Khafif**

24. What is the name of the poem, which was formed directly in Turkish literature, is written in the musad of strict ramali in maqsur weight, consists of four lines, and at the end of the line, radifs consist of homonymous words? – **Tuyuq**

25. What is the name of the change of the Ramal sea (VV - -)? – **Mahbun**

BILET #4

1–question. Determine the following weight of Alisher Navoi. Look at my eyes, come and do science, make a country like a people under my eyes. B – B – / VV – – / B – B – / – – (**Mujtassi musamli mahbuni maqtu'**)

2. Analyze the following verse of Babur's Rubaiyat. Sarrishtayi aishdin kunkul zinhor, Uz oh, Zahiridin Muhammad Babur. **Hazaji musamuli akhrabi maqbuzi salimi azall**

3. What is the name of Mustafilun asli's mafailun zihof? - mahbun 4. Who first used the term "poetics"? - **Aristotle**

5. What is the name of a poem written in two languages in a certain order? - **Shiru-shakar**

6. What is the name of the farm of Hazaj Bay? - maqbuz

7. Identify Furqat's scientific work, which was compiled as a guide for literature lovers, and describes the rules of aruz weight. - **"Ilmi Ash'ar's rule of law"**

8. What is the result of the repetition of Failotun and Mustafilun? - **Khafif**

9. What is the name of the lyrical genre in a solemn style that praises famous historical figures and great events? - **poem**

10. What is the name of Babur's work dedicated to the science of aruz? - **"Mukhtasar"**

11. Which original column is not created from repetition? - **mafolotu**

12. In which book was the first ghazal in Turkish? - **Ramal**

13. What is the name of the fo' (~) zihof of the original Mafoiylun? - **Azall**

14. Write down the 5th stanza of Ogahi's ghazal, which begins with

"The jury of Mushkin Koshi...".

She is a flower-faced soul with

the noise of the night and the morning.

Like a nightingale, she sings a hundred and a thousand kinds of cries.

15. What is the name of failon (VV ~) of the root of foilotun? - **mahbuni mahzuf** 16. In which season was Navoi's work "Hayratu-l-abror" created? - **sari'**

17. Which of the "Khamsa" epics was created in Mutaqarib Bahr? - **"Saddi Iskandarii"**

18. What is the name of a riddle-poem that consists of one stanza, sometimes two-three stanzas, written on the basis of an emphasis or hint, which relies on hiding something through Arabic letters? – **Problem**

19. What is the name of the art of referring to famous historical events, legends, literary works or proverbs in poetry or prose? - **Talmih**

20. What is the name of a poem with seven verses in each stanza? - **Musabba'**.

21. The nightingale is crying and the dawn is dawning, drinking blood like a bud, and a hundred and seven flowers are wearing it. What poetic art did Furqat use in this verse? - **Husni Talil**

22. What is the result of repetition of Mutafailun Rukni? – **komil**

23. What is the name of poetic art based on homonymous words? – **Tajnis**

24. What is the name of Mustafilun (– –V ~) of the original Mustafilun? - **muzol** 25. What is the name of a poem with three verses in each stanza? - **You're welcome.**

TICKET #5

1. Determine the weight of Alisher Navoi below.

    My parting is like night and morning,

    There is no possibility of this type of night and morning. B – B – / VV – – / B – B – / – – (**Mujtassi musamli mahbuni maktu'**)

2. Determine the weight of Alisher Navoi below. There is no bush like you, Chin aro, Buti Chin is your slave. B – – /B – – / B – – / B – (**Mutaqaribi musamuli mahzuf**)

3. What is the name of the poem with six verses in each stanza? - **Musaddas**.

4. What is the name of the property of Hazaj Bay? - **maqsur**

5. What is the name of a poem that was formed directly in Turkish literature, is written in maqsur weight, consists of four lines, and consists of radifs homonymous words at the end of the line? – Tuyuq

6. What is the name of the muftailun zihof of

Mustafilun Asli? - **matvii**

7. What is the name of the art of proving an image or situation with something else that has nothing to do with it, giving a beautiful reason, even if it is a lie? – **Husni Talil**

8. Which type of science is an Arabic compound meaning the science of beautiful speech, rare, wonderful expression? - **Ilmi badi'**

9. Mustafilun, what is the result of repetition of activities? - **Mujtass**

10. What is the name of the art of providing a reason for an event depicted in literary works? - **husni talil**

11. What is the name of the art based on giving an example of a life event in the second verse as evidence for the idea expressed in the first verse of the poem? – **Tamsil**

12. What is the result of the repetition of Mustafilun, Maf'alotu? - **Munsarih**

13. What is the name of a lyrical poem that expresses grief over someone's death? – **Marcia**

14. What is the result of repetition of Mafailatun

column? – **wafir**

15. What is the name of the so-and-so (– ~) root of foilotun? – **musabbag'**

16. Who is the author of the work "Badoyi' us-sanoyi"? - **Atullah Hosseini**

17. What genre did Alisher Navoi describe as "Vase' Maidan" in the treatise "Mezan ul-Avzon"? - **masnawi**

18. This art involves first mentioning the names of several things or concepts (similes) in a verse, and then successively stating judgments (similes) about them. What art is it about? - **Laff and publication**

19. What is the result of the repetition of Mustaf'ilun, Mustaf'ilun, Ma'afulatu? – Sari' 20. What is the name of the lyrical genre in a solemn style that praises famous historical figures and great events? - **poem**

21. What is the name of Navoi's work dedicated to the science of aruz? - **"Mezonu-l-avzon"**

22. Which original verse does not benefit from the exact repetition? - **mafolotu** 23. Who wrote

the first Turkish ghazal? – **Rabguzi**

24. What is the name of the root of Mafoiylun (- V -)? – **ashtar**

25. Which lyrical genre is the first to be placed in the creation of a divan by its nature? – **Gazal**

TICKET #6

1. Determine the weight of the following stanza by Alisher Navoi.

Haili is the eloquent head officer,
Ganji is the jewel of the close officer. –
VV – / – VV – / – V – **Sariyi musaddasi matviyi makshuf**

2. I came into the world and fell into the mud, I swallowed the poison of no medicine. (Mashrab) Define byte weight. – – V / V – – V / V – – V / V – – (**Hazaji musmali akhrabi makfufi mahzuf**)

3. What is the name of failun (VV –) root of Failotun? - **mahbuni mahzuf**

4. What is the name of the smallest one-stanza poem in classical literature? - **Fard** 5. What is it called to refer to historical events and persons, literary heroes in poetry? - **talmeh** ("to look")

6. What is the result of the repetition of foilotun, mustafilun? - **Khafif**

7. What effect is formed from the repetition of Mutafailun Rukni? - **komil**

8. Mustafilun, what is the result of repetition of the activity? – **Mujtass**

9. What is the name of Furqat's work dedicated to Aruz weight? - **"Ilmi Ashor's rule of thumb"**

10. Which juzv does the form (V -) belong to? - **watadi majmu'**

11. In which poetic art can elements such as means and basis be found? - **tashbih** 12. In what season was Navoi's work "Farhad and Shirin" created? - **Hazaji musaddasi mahzuf**

13. What is the result of the repetition of foilotun and mustafilun? - **Khafif**

14. What is the name of a poem that can be read both horizontally and vertically? - **masnu'**

15. What is the name of the change in the temperature of Ramal sea (VV - V)? – **Mashkul**

16. What is the name of the art of poetically showing some reason for an event described in literary works? - **husni talil**

17. What is the name of the art based on giving an example of a life event in the second verse as evidence for the idea expressed in the first verse

of the poem? - **Tamsil**

18. What is the result of the repetition of Mustaf'ilun, maf'alotu? - **Munsarih**

19. What is the name of a lyrical poem that expresses grief over someone's death? - **Marcia**

20. What is the result of repetition of Mafailatun column? – **wafer**

21. What is the name of fa'lun (– –) of the root of foilotun? - **maqtu**

22. Who is the author of "Badoyi'u-s-sanoyi"? - **Atullah Hosseini**

23. What genre did Alisher Navoi describe as "Vase' Maidan" in the treatise "Mezan ul-Avzon"? - **masnavi**

24. What is the name of poetic art based on alphabetic calculation? - **history**

25. In what sea was the first Turkish epic created? – **Mutaqarib**

TICKET #7

1. Determine the weight of the following stanza by Alisher Navoi.

    It is a dilgir in the ring of the chain,
    It is a chain with a sound.

    Don't tell me, my skirt is a tulip,
    Kim, the skirt of my pain is a tulip. – – V / – V – V / V – – V / – V – (**Muzore'i musamali akhrabi makfufi mahzuf**)

3. What is the name of such-and-such (– ~) zihof of the root of foilotun? - **maktuyi musabbagh`**

4. Who is the author of the work "Badoyi' us-sanoyi'"? - **Atullah Husayniy**

5. If a person has even an iota of love, he will cry. What kind of image is the combination highlighted in the stanza? – **metaphor**

6. What is the name of Babur's work dedicated to the science of aruz? - **"Brief"**

7. To which juzv does the form (VVV -) belong? - **Fasilayi kubro**

8. What is the name of the root fo' (~) of

Mafoiylun? - **Azall**

9. What is the name of the lyrical genre in a ceremonial style that praises famous historical figures and great events? **Qasida**

10. What is the name of the home of the Hazaj Bay? - **maqbuz**

11. What is the name of the root of foiloton (VV - ~)? - **mahbuni musabbag'**

12. Life is tight to someone, open to someone is death. What is the name of the type of rhyming of opposite words? – **Contrast rhyme**

13. What is the name of the rhyming type of rubai in the order a+a+a+a? - **taronai ruboiy**

14. What is the name of the art of referring to famous historical events, legends, literary works or proverbs in poetry or prose? - **Talmih**

15. What is the name of the mafailun zihof of Mustafilun asli? - **mahbun**

16. What is the name of the change of sea of Ramal (- V ~)? - **Maqsur**

17. What is the name of the faulun afoyil of Hazaj

Bay? - **mahzuf**

18. Each volume is equal to a ghazal and is a poem composed of stanzas that rhyme like a ghazal, in which the two lines at the end of each stanza have an independent melody. What lyrical genre are we talking about? – **Tarkibband**

19. What is the name of the art of poetically showing some reason for an event described in literary works? - **husni talil**

20. What is the name of the change in the activity of the Ramal sea (– V – V)? – **Makfuf**

21. What is the name of the art based on giving an example of a life event in the second verse as evidence for the idea expressed in the first verse of the poem? – **tamsil**

23. What is the name of the poetic art based on alphabet calculation? – **history**

24. Sunbul-u is a flower bud, no doubt about it, Zulf-u is dying because of his face. (Gadoiy) Which poetic art is expressed through the highlighted words in this stanza? - **Laff and nashr**

25. You, O flower, did not let go of your swaying like a cypress, I begged you to fall at your feet like a leaf. (Babur) What kind of poetic art is expressed in this stanza by using the word "flower" in the human sense? – **Metaphor**

TICKET #8

1. Determine the byte weight.
   My head is a storehouse, a young girl in my soul,
   Your eyes are searching, a girl with a fishy face. (Mashrab) –V – / V – – – / –V – / V – – – **Hazaji musamoli ashtar**

2. Determine the weight of the following ghazali by Alisher Navoi. The weather was nice and I had a glass of beer, I was drinking a glass of wine. V – V – / VV – – / V – V – / VV ~ **(Mujtassi kusamoli mahbuni maksur)**

3. When your arrows hit my heart, both my eyes and my body burned. (Navoi) What poetic art is expressed through the second line of the verse? - h**ereditary parable**

4. What is the name of the art of poetically showing some reason for an event described in literary works? - **Husni Talil**

5. What is the name of a form of poetry with ten verses in each stanza? – **Muashshar**

6. What is the name of a four-line poem on romantic, moral, political-philosophical themes,

which is widely used in Uzbek classical literature, written in the Akhram and Akhrab genealogies of Hazaj Bahr? – **Rubaiyi**

7. What is the name of a ghazal if the second verse is rhymed in addition to the first verse? - **Ghazali husni matla'**

8. How many ghazals are included in Alisher Navoi's work "Khazayin ul-Ma'ani"? - **2600**

9. Whoever wishes to kill the highest, know the Kishilikdin well.

Superiority in the killing ranks Know better in the killing ranks.

Identify the genre of poetry written by Navoi. – **Qit'a**

10. According to the tradition of devon composition, which lyrical genre is included at the end of the devon? - **fard**

11. A lover is faithful in his work.

A lover is a lover in the beginning. What type of classic rhyme is used in the stanza? - **muqayyad rhyme**

12. In his book "Literary Rules" for the first time comprehensive information is given about the uniqueness of fiction, social nature, literary types and genres, subject, composition, artistic speech and skills. Which scientist are we talking about here? - **Fitrat**

13. What is the name of Sheikh Ahmed Tarazi's work dedicated to classical poetics? - **"Funun ul-baloga"**

14. What is the result of repetition of Mafailatun verse? – **wafer**

15. What is the name of fa'lun (– –) of the root of foilotun? - **maqtu**

16. Who is the author of "Badoyi'u-s-sanoyi"? - **Atullah Hosseini**

17. What genre did Alisher Navoi describe as "Vase' Maidan" in the treatise "Mezan ul-Avzon"? **- masnavi**

18. What is the name of the poetic art based on alphabetic calculation? **- history** 19. In which sea was the first Turkish epic created? - **Mutaqarib**

20. If a poet writes a mukhammas completely by

himself, which type of mukhammas does it belong to? - **tabi khud muhammas (muhammasi tabi khud)** 21. Who emphasized tuyuq as "a characteristic of Turkish shuara"? - **A.Navoi**

22. A form of poetry with a rhyming structure similar to that of a stanza. The difference is that if one stanza at the end of the stanza rhymes independently, the same stanza is repeated at the end of all stanzas. What genre is it about? - **Tarje'band**

23. In Uzbek literature, which poet is described as "the perfect inventor"? - to **Ogahii**

24. What is the name of Mustafilun Asli's mafailun zihof? - **mahbun**

25. What is the name of the change in the sea of Ramal (- V ~)? – **Faulty**

TICKET #9

1. Determine the weight of Alisher Navoi below. There is no one who is loyal to me like you, and there is no one who is loyal to you like me. – – V / V – – V / V – – V / V – – (**Hazaji musmali akhrabi makfufi mahzuf**)

2. Fasli navbahor is dead, secretary winters, Friends, it's a spoil, go for a walk, gulistans. Define byte weight. –V – / V – – – / –V – / V – – – **Hazaji musmali ashtar**

3. What is the name of the art of referring to famous historical events, legends, literary works or proverbs in poetry or prose? - **Talmih**

4. What is the name of the mafailun zihof of Mustafilun asli? – **mahbun**

5. What is the name of the change of Ramal sea (- V ~)? - **Maqsur**

6. What is the name of the faulun afoyil of Hazaj Bay? - **mahzuf**

7. Each volume is equal to a ghazal and is a poem made up of stanzas that rhyme like a ghazal, in

which the two lines at the end of each stanza have an independent melody. What lyrical genre are we talking about? – **Tarkibband**

8. What is the name of the art of using words with opposite meanings in a verse? - **Tazad**

9. My drops of blood poured down on my chest, I don't mean it's a pity, blood is crying over my condition. (Navoi) Find out what kind of art is used based on the general content of the verse. - **Husni Talil**

10. Its dictionary meaning is "fragment, piece, part" and pandnama is written in an educational spirit. It will consist of at least two bytes. In rhyming, the odd verses are left open, and the even verses rhyme with each other (б–а, в–а, г–а...). What genre is it about? – **Qit'a**

11. What is the result of repetition of Mafailatun column? – **wafir**

12. What is the name of fa'lun (– –) of the root of foilotun? – **maq'tu**

13. What is the name of the change in the activity of Ramal sea (- V - V)? - **Makfuf**

14. What is the name of the art based on giving an example of a life event in the second verse as evidence for the idea expressed in the first verse of the poem? – **Tamsil**

15. What is the name of the poetic art based on alphabet calculation? - **history**

16. Who is the author of "Badoyi'u-s-sanoyi"? - **Atullah Hosseini**

17. What is the name of Sheikh Ahmad Tarazi's work on classical poetics? - **"Funun ul-baloga"**

18. In this form of art, a new word is created using the letters of the Arabic alphabet. What art is it about? - **extraction**

19. What is the name of a rhyme that occurs in more than two rhyme styles, but the lines are not completely rhymed? - **Zulqavafi'**

20. What is the name of the smallest one-stanza poem in classical literature? - **Fard** 21. What is the rhyming type of rubai in the order a+a+b+a usually called? - Khosayi (ordinary) **Rubaiy**

22. What is the name of the lyrical genre in a solemn style that praises famous historical figures

and great events? - **Qasida**

23. What is the result of the repetition of foilotun and mustafilun? - **Khafif**

24. What is the result of the repetition of Mustaf'ilun, maf'alotu? - **Munsarih**

25. What is the name of the art of providing a poetic reason for an event described in literary works? – **Husni ta'lil**

Ticket 103#

1. Determine the weight of the following verse by Alisher Navoi.
   Haili is the eloquent head officer,
   Ganji is the jewel of the close officer.
   – VV – / – VV – / – V – **Sariyi musaddasi matviyi makshuf**

2. Determine the weight of the following ghazali by Alisher Navoi. My parting is like night and morning, There is no possibility of this type of night and morning. V – V – / VV – – / V – V – / – – **(Mujtassi kusamli mahbuni maqtu')**

3. What is the name of the original (VV – ~) zihof of foilatun? - **mahbuni musabbagh**

4. What is the name of the smallest one-stanza poem in classical literature? - **Fard** 5. It is a poem composed of stanzas, each equal in size to a ghazal and rhyming like a ghazal, in which the two lines at the end of each stanza have an independent melody. What lyrical genre are we talking about? – **Tarkibband**

6. What is the result of the repetition of foilotun and mustafilun? - **Khafif**

7. Which effect is formed from the repetition of Mutafailun Rukni? - **komil**

8. Mustafilun, what is the result of repetition of the activity? **- Mujtass**

9. What is the name of Furqat's work dedicated to Aruz weight? - **"Ilmi Ashor's rule of thumb**"

10. Which juzv does the form (V -) belong to? - **watadi majmu'**

11. In which poetic art can elements such as means and basis be found? **- tashbih** 12. Life is hard for someone, and death is death for someone. What is the name of using opposite words as a rhyme? **– Contrast rhyme**

13. What is the name of the rhyming type of rubai in the order a+a+a+a? - **Taronayi Rubaiy**

14. What is the name of the art of referring to famous historical events, legends, literary works or proverbs in poetry or prose? - **Talmih**

15. What is the name of the mafailun zihof of Mustafilun Asli? **- mahbun**

16. What is the name of the change of Ramal Bay (- V ~)? - **Maqsur**

17. What is the name of the faulun afoyil of Hazaj Bay? – **mahzuf**

18. Each volume is equal to a ghazal and is a poem composed of stanzas that rhyme like a ghazal, in which the two lines at the end of each stanza have an independent melody. What lyrical genre are we talking about? – **Tarkibband**

19. What is the name of the art of poetically showing some reason for an event described in literary works? - **husni talil**

20. What is the name of the change in the activity of Ramal sea (– V – V)? - **Makfuf**

21. What is the name of the art based on giving an example of a life event in the second verse as evidence for the idea expressed in the first verse of the poem? – **Tamsil**

23. What is the name of the poetic art based on alphabet calculation? - **history**

24. Sunbul-u is a flower bud, no doubt about it, Zulf-u is dying because of his face. (Gadoiy) Which poetic art is expressed through the highlighted words in this stanza? - **Laff and nashr**

25. You, O flower, did not let go of your swaying like a cypress, I begged you to fall at your feet like a leaf. (Babur) What kind of poetic art is expressed in this stanza by using the word "flower" in the human sense? – **Metaphor**

TICKET No. 11

1. Write and analyze the weight of Babur's ghazal praise, which begins with
"The sale of his hair has fallen"
   I used to walk like Babur until my feet stopped,
   but the trade of Sochi started to fall again. (– B – – / (– B – – /(– B – – /(– B –)
   Ramali musmali mahzuf

2. Determine the weight of Alisher Navoi's following ghazali.
   His head began to turn white and his teeth began to fall out.) work. V – V – – / V – V – / VV – (**Mujtassi mahbuni mahzuf**)

3. What is the name of the poem consisting of ten verses?**Muashshar**

5. It is one of the spiritual arts, and at the same time, the poem is written in the form of a ghazal What is it about? - **Muvashshah**

6. What is the result of repeating the verb? What is the name of the poem? - **Tuyuq**

8. What is the name of a riddle-poem that consists

of one stanza, sometimes two-three stanzas, and is based on an emphasis or a hint that hides something through Arabic letters? - **Problem**

9. What is the name of the muftailun zihof of Mustafilun Asli? - **matvii**

10. What is the name of the art of poetically showing some reason for an event described in literary works? - **husni ta'lil**

11. A lover is faithful in his work, a lover is a lover in the beginning. What type of classic rhyme is used in the stanza? - **muqayyad rhyme**

12. In his book "Literary Rules" for the first time comprehensive information is given about the uniqueness of fiction, social nature, literary types and genres, subject, composition, artistic speech and skills. Which scientist are we talking about here? - **Fitrat**

13. What is the name of Sheikh Ahmed Tarazi's work dedicated to classical poetics? - **"Funun ul-baloga"**

14. What is the result of repetition of Mafailatun verse? – **wafir**

15. What is the name of fa'lun (– –) of the root of foilotun? – **maq'tu**

16. Who is the author of "Badoyi'u-s-sanoyi"? - **Atullah Hosseini**

17. What genre did Alisher Navoi describe as "Vase' Maidan" in the treatise "Mezan ul-Avzon"? - **masna**vi

18. What is the name of the poetic art based on alphabetic calculation? - **history** 19. In what sea was the first Turkish epic created? – **Mutaqarib**

20. If a poet writes a mukhammas completely by himself, which type of mukhammas does it belong to? – **tab'i khud mukhammas (mukhammasi tab'i khud)**

21. What is the name of the change of Ramal Bay to Foilon (– V ~)? - **Maqsu**r

22. This genre gives the impression of being taken from a ghazal. The difference from the ghazal is the absence of the matla' part. What genre is it about? – **Qit'a**

23. Who is the poet who wrote the most ghazals in Turkish? - **A.Navoi**

24. What is the name of Mustafilun's main residence? – **mahbun**

25. In Uzbek literature, which poet is described as "a perfect inventor"? - **To Ogahi**

TICKET #12

1. Determine the weight of the following byte of Babur.

    In my life, I have not found a loyal friend,
    and in my heart I have not found a secret wife. – – V / – V – V / V – – V / – V – **(Muzore'i musmali akhrabi makfufi mahzuf)**

2. Determine the weight by writing down the second stanza of Ogahi's ghazal beginning with "Mushkin Koshi's Hayat...".

    The beauty of the beauty of the spectacle is combined,
    if you don't see it, the graft of the flower is on the candlestick. – – V – / – – V – / – – V – / – – V – **Rajazi musammani solim**

3. Analyze the weight of the following Ruba'i verse. Munis, demand perfection - you will grow up, young man, - - V / V - V - / V - - V / V - **Hazaji musammani akhrabi maqbuzi makfufi ajabb**

4. Sunbul-he is a flower bud, no doubt

about it,

Zulf-he died because of his face . (Gadoiy) Which poetic art is expressed through the highlighted words in this stanza? - **Laff and nashr**

5. You, O flower, did not stop your swaying like a cypress tree,

I begged you to fall at your feet like a leaf. (Babur)

What kind of poetic art is expressed in this stanza by using the word "flower" in the human sense? – **Istiora**

6. "-V" pattern belongs to which part? – **watadi mafruk**

7. What is the name of the fauvlun (V – –) zihof of the original Mafoiylun? – **mahzuf**

8. Who created the book "Rules of Literature" which is considered to be a truly comprehensive scientific work on the theory of literature in Uzbek literature in the 20s of the 20th century? – **Fitrat**

9. What is the name of the lyrical genre in a

solemn style that praises famous historical figures and great events? **Qasida**

10. What is the name of the mafailun afoyil of Hazaj Bay? – **maqbuz**

11. What is the name of the root of foiloton (VV - ~)? - **mahbuni musabbag'**

12. Who is the author of the manual "Learning Aruz weight at school" published by "Teacher" publishing house in 1995? - **A. Hojiahmedov**

13. What are the last sounds at the end of rhyming root words and the base of artificial words called? - **Ravi**

14. If someone blames you, don't worry, the mirror has become cloudy. According to the convention of devon, identify this genre to be included at the end of the devon. - **fard**

15. How many ghazals are included in "Khazayin ul-ma'ani" collection of Alisher Navoi, who wrote the most ghazals in the Turkish language? - **2600 16**.

16.What is the name of the sea of Hazaj? – **mahzuf**

17. Where do the elements of tasis, ridf, note, dahl come in the rhyme? - **Before Ravi**

18. Which lyrical genre is described as "pure Turkish"? - **tuyuq**

19. What is the name of the art of poetically showing some reason for an event described in literary works? - **husni talil**

20. What is the name of the change in the activity of the Ramal sea (– V – V)? - Makfuf 21. What is the name of the change of the original mafaiylun to mafailun (V - V -)? - **maqbuz**

22. What is the name of the change of the original mafoiylun to mafoiylon (V - - ~)? – **musabbag'**

23. What is the name of the change of the root of the root to so-and-so (- ~)? - **maqtu'i musabbagh'**

24. What is the name of the change of the original foilun (-V-)? – mahzuf 25. What is the name of the change of failun (VV –) of the root of foilotun? - **mahbuni mahzuf**

TICKET #13

1. Determine the weight of the following piece of cloth by Alisher Navoi.
   There is no one who is loyal to me like you,
   and there is no one who is loyal to you like me. – – V / V – – V / V – – V / V – –
   (**Hazaji musmali akhrabi makfufi mahzuf**)

2. Fasli navbahor is dead, secretary winters,
   Friends, it's a spoil, go for a walk, gulistans. Define byte weight. –V – / V – – – / –V – / V – – – **Hazaji musmali ashtar**

3. What is the name of the fauvl (V ~) change of the original fauvlun? – **maqsur** 4. What is the name of the change of the original mafoiylun to failun (– V –)? – **ashtar**

5. What is the active (V –) change of the original Mafoiylun called? – **ajab**

6. Who is the author of "Badoyi'u-s-sanoyi"? - **Atullah Hosseini**

7. What genre did Alisher Navoi describe as "Vase' Maidan" in the treatise "Mezan ul-Avzon"? – **masnavi**

8. What is the name of the poetic art based on alphabet calculation? - **history**

9. In what sea was the first Turkish epic created? – mutaqarib

10. What is the name of the change of the root of the verb to the form of the verb (– V – ~)? - **musabbagh**

11. What is the name of the art based on giving an example of a life event in the second verse as evidence for the idea expressed in the first verse of the poem? - **Tamsil**

12. What is the result of the repetition of Mustafilun, Ma'afulatu? – **Munsarih**

13. What is the name of a lyrical poem that expresses grief over someone's death? - **Marcia**

14. What is the result of repetition of Mafailatun column? – **vofir**

15. What is the name of the change of fauvlun to fauvl (V ~)? - **maqsur**

16. In what sea was Navoi's work "Hayratu-l-abror" created? - **sari'**

17. Which of the "Khamsa" epics was created in Mutaqarib Bahr? - **"Saddi Iskandarii"**

18. What is the name of a riddle-poem that consists of one stanza, sometimes two-three stanzas, written on the basis of an emphasis or hint, which relies on hiding something through Arabic letters? - **Problem**

19. What is the name of the art of referring to famous historical events, legends, literary works or proverbs in poetry or prose? - **Talmih**

20. What is the name of the change of fa'lun (– –) of the original fawlun? - **aslam** 21. What is the name of the change of the original mafoiylun to mafoiyl (V - ~)? – **maqsur**

22. What is the name of the change of the original mafoiylun to maf'ulun (– – –)? - **akhram**

23. What is the name of the change of the original fauvlun to faulu (V - V)? – **maqbuz**

24. What is the name of the change of the original Mustafilun to mafailun (V – V –)? –

mahbun

25. What is the name of the change of the original mustafilun to muftailun (VV –)? – **matviy**

TICKET #14

1. Determine the weight of the following piece of cloth by Alisher Navoi.

   Wake up your two beautiful girls from their sweet sleep,
   Play in the flower garden until they fall asleep. – – V / V – – – / – – V / V – – – **(Khazaji musammani akhrab)**

2. Determine the weight of the following verse of Alisher Navoi.

   Haili is the eloquent head officer,
   Ganji is the jewel of the close officer. (– VV – / – VV – / – V –) **Sariyi musaddasi matviyi makshuf**

3. What is the name of the mafoiyl (V – ~) change of the original fauvlun? – **musabbagh**

4. What is the name of the change of the original mustafilun to mafailun (V – V –)? – **mahbun**

5. What is the name of the change of the original mafoiylun to mafoilun (V – V –)? – **maqbuz**

6. What is the name of the change of the root of the root (-V-V)? – **makfuf**

7. What is the name of the change of fauvlun to fauvl (V ~)? – **maqsur**

8. What is the name of the change of the original mustafilun to muftailun (VV –)? – **matviy**

9. What is the name of the change of mustafilun (– – V ~) of the original mustafilun? - **muzol**

10. What is the name of the change of the original mafoiylun to failun (- V -)? – **ashtar**

11. What is the name of failoton (VV – ~) of the root of foilotun? - **mahbuni musabbag'**

12. Life is tight to someone, open to someone is death. What is the name of using opposite words as a rhyme? – **Contrast rhyme**

13. What is the name of the rhyming type of rubai in the order a+a+a+a? - **Taronayi Rubaiy**

14. What is the name of the art of referring to famous historical events, legends, literary works or proverbs in poetry or prose? - **Talmih**

15. What is the name of the change of the root

mafoiylun to faulun (V - -)? – **mahzuf**

16. What is the name of the change of Ramal sea (– V ~)? - **Maqsur**

17. What is the name of the faulun afoyil of Hazaj Bay? - **mahzuf**

18. This genre was used for the first time in the Turkish language in the "Qissayi Yusuf" part of Rabguzi's "Qisasi Rabguzi". What lyrical genre are we talking about? **- Ghazal**

19. What is the name of the art of poetically showing some reason for an event described in literary works? **- husni talil**

20. What is the name of the change in the activity of the Ramal sea (– V – V)? – **Makfuf**

21. In the science of rhyme, where are the elements of wasl, khuruj, mazid, noyira located? - **after the narrator**

22. What is the active (V -) change of the Fauvlun root called? – **mahzuf**

23. What is the name of the change of the original mustafilun to mafailon (V – V ~)? - **mahbuni muzol**

24. What is the name of the change of the original mafoiylun to mafoiylu (V - - V)? – **makfuf**

25. What is the name of the change of the root of foilotun to so-and-so (– ~)? – maq'tui musabbag'

TICKET #15

1. Determine the weight of the following stanza by Alisher Navoi.

    It is a dilgir in the ring of the chain,
    It is a chain with a sound.
    Don't tell me, my skirt is a tulip,
    Kim, the skirt of my pain is a tulip. – – V / – V – V / V – – V / – V – (**Muzore'i musmali akhrabi makfufi mahzuf**)

    3. What is the name of the change of the original mafoiylun to mafoiylon (V – – ~)? – **musabbag**

    4. What is the name of the change of the original mafoiylun to mafoilun (V - V -)? – **maqbuz**

    5. What is the name of the change of the original verb (VV - ~)? - **mahbuni musabbag'**

    6. What is the name of the change of the root of foilotun to foilato (-V-V)? - **makfuf**

    7. Each volume is equal to a ghazal and is a poem composed of stanzas that rhyme like a ghazal, in

which the two verses at the end of each stanza have an independent melodiousness. What lyrical genre are we talking about? - **Tarkibband**

8. What is the name of the art of using words with opposite meanings in a verse? – **Tazad**

9. My drops of blood poured down on my chest

I don't mean it's a pity, blood is crying over my condition. (Navoi) Find out what art is used based on the general content of the verse. - **Husni Talil**

10. Its dictionary meaning is "fragment, fragment, part" and pandnama is written in an educational spirit. It will consist of at least two bytes. In rhyming, the odd verses are left open, and the even verses rhyme with each other (б–а, в–а, г–а...). What genre is it about? – **Qit'a**

11. What is the name of the change of fauvlun to faulu (V – V)? – **maqbuz**

12. What is the name of the change of the original mustafilun to mafailun (V – V –)? – **mahbun**

13. What is the name of the change of the

original mafoiylun to mafoiyl (V - ~)? – **maqsur**

14. What is the name of the change of the original mafoiylun to failun (– V –)? – **ashta**r

15. What is the name of the change of Mustafilun to Mustafilan (– – V ~)? - **muzol**

16. What is the name of the change of the root of the word "Foilatun" (- V - ~)? – **musabbag**'

17. What is the name of the change of the original foilotun to failotun (VV - -)? – **Makhbun**

18. What is the name of falun (– –) change of the original Failotun? – **maktu'**

19. What is the name of the change of the root of the root to so-and-so (– ~)? – **maqtu'i musabbagh'**

20. What is the name of the change of the root of Fauvlun to mafoiyl (V - ~)? – **musabbagh**

21. What is the name of the change of fauvlun to fauvl (V ~)? – **maqsur**

22. What is the name of the change of the original mafoiylun to mafoiylu (V – – V)? – **makfuf**

23. What is the name of the change of the original

62

mafoiylun to maf'ulun (– – –)? - **akhram**

24. What is the name of the change of the root of foilotun to foilon (- V ~)? – **maqsu**r

25. What is the name of the change of the original mustafilun to mafailon (V – V ~)? - **mahbuni muzol**

TICKET #16

1. Determine the weight of the following piece of cloth by Alisher Navoi. There is no bush like you, Chin aro, Buti Chin is your slave. V – – /V – – / - – – / V – (**Mutaqaribi musmuli mahzuf**)

2. Determine the weight of the following ghazali of Alisher Navoi.

My parting is like night and morning,

There is no possibility of this type of night and morning. V – V – / VV – – / V – V – / – – (**Mujtassi kusamli mahbuni maktu'**)

3. What is the name of the mosque of the Hazaj Bay? – **maksur**

4. What is the name of a poem with six lines in each stanza? – **Musaddas**.

5. What is the art of using words or groups of words that have the same form but different meanings in speech? — **Tajnis**

6. Mustafilun, what is the result of repetition of activities? - **Mujtass**

7. The jury of Mushkin's eye ul chashmi jallad ustina brings "nas" for execution "nun" eltiban "sad" ustina. (Note) What poetic art is used in this stanza? – **kitoba**t

8. What is the name of a poem that was formed directly in Turkish literature, is written in strict ramali musadad in maqsur weight, consists of four lines, and at the end of the line, radifs consist of homonymous words? – **Tuyuq**

9. What is the name of the muftailun zihof of Mustafilun Asli? - **matviy**

10. What is the name of the art of poetically showing some reason for an event described in literary works? - **husni talil**

11. What is the name of the art based on giving an example of a life event in the second verse as evidence for the idea expressed in the first verse of the poem? - **Tamsi**l

12. What is the result of the repetition of Mustafilun, Maf'alotu? – **Munsarih**

13. What is the name of a lyrical poem that

expresses grief in connection with the death of a person? – **Marcia**

14. What is the name of the so-and-so (– ~) root of the root of foilotun? - maktuyi **musabbag**h

15. What is the result of repetition of Mafailatun verse? - **Vafir**

16. Who is the author of the work "Badoyi' us-sanoyi"? - **Atullah Hosseini**

17. What is the name of the art of proving an image or situation with something unrelated to it, giving a beautiful reason, even if it is a lie? - **Husni Talil**

18. What genre did Alisher Navoi describe as "Vase' Maidan" in the treatise "Mezan ul-Avzon"? - **masnavi**

19. What is the result of the repetition of Mustafilun, Mustafilun, and Ma'falotu? – **Sari'**

20. What is the name of the lyrical genre in a solemn style that praises famous historical figures and great events? - **QASIDA**

21. Which lyrical genre is placed first in the creation of a devan according to its nature? -

Ghazal

22. What is the exact repetition of the original verse that does not produce benefit? - **mafolotu**

23. Who wrote the first Turkish ghazal? – **Rabguz**i

24. What is the name of the root of Mafoiylun (- V -)? – **ashta**r

25. What is the name of Navoi's work dedicated to the science of aruz? - **"Mezonu-l-avzon"**

TICKET #17

1. Determine the weight of the following byte of Babur.

    If he comes, I won't be disloyal. – – V / – V – V / V – – V / – V – (**Muzore'i musammani akhrabi makfufi mahzuf**)

2. Determine the weight of the following verse of Babur.

    Disappointed with a wonderful prom dress,

    Shikasta is disappointed with a black prom dress. V – V – / VV – – / V – V – / – – (**Mujtassi musammani maxbuni maqtu'**)

3. What is the name of a ghazal with an internal rhyme? - **Ghazali musajja'**

4. What is the name of a poem with nine verses in each stanza? – **muxtassa**.

5. What is the name of a poem written in two languages in a certain order? - **Shiru-shakar**

6. What is the name of the farm of Hazaj Bay? – **maqbuz**

7. Make the faces of creatures,

Latofat mus'hafiga Oya Navruz. What kind of poetic arts are used in this verse belonging to the Agahi style? - **tashbeh, diagnosis**

8. Which result is formed from the repetition of foilotun and mustafilun? - **Khafif** 9. One morning I was awake: the world was burning with fire, the mountains were smoking and trembling, the deserts were shaking. What poetic art did Furqat use in this verse? – **Revitalization**

10. What is the name of the change of the sea of Ramal (VV - -)? – **Makhbun**

11. What is the name of Mustafilun's main residence? - **mahbun**

12. Who first used the term "Poetics"? - **Aristotle**

13. In the stanza, the words that are placed on top of each other in the verses are balanced, melodic and rhyming. What kind of poetic art are you talking about? - **Tarse'**

14. What is the result of the repetition of Mustaf'ilun, Mustafilun, Ma'afulatu? -**Sari'**

15. What is the result of the repetition of mafaiylun, failotun? - **Muzori'**

16. What is the name of a riddle-poem that consists of one stanza, sometimes two-three stanzas, written on the basis of an emphasis or hint, which relies on hiding something through Arabic letters? – **Problem**

17. What is the name of a poem with seven verses in each stanza? - **Musabba'**.

18. Mustafilun, what is the result of repeating an activity? - **Mujtass**

19. Which bahr is formed from the repetition of Mafailatun verse? – **Wafir**

20. What is the name of the art of referring to famous historical events, legends, literary works or proverbs in poetry or prose? – **Talmih**

21. What is the name of a four-line poem on romantic, moral, political-philosophical topics, which is widely used in Uzbek classical literature, written in the Akhram and Akhrab genealogies of Hazaj Bahr? - **Ruba'i**

22. Mustaf'ilun, what is the result of repetition of maf'alotu? – **Munsarih**

23. What is the name of the art of providing a

poetic reason for an event described in literary works? - **husni talil**

24. What is the name of the art based on giving an example of a life event in the second verse as evidence for the idea expressed in the first verse of the poem? – **Tamsil**

25. What is the name of the art of quoting a folk proverb to prove a point expressed in poetry and prose? - **Irsoli masal**

TICKET #18

1. Determine the weight of the following piece of cloth by Alisher Navoi. Look at my eyes, come and do science, make a country like a people under my eyes. B – B – / VV – – / B – B – / – – **(Mujtassi musammani mahbuni maktu')**

2. Determine the weight of the following verse of Babur.

        Hajjr of the month of Ghurbat made me old,

        Hijran and Ghurbat affected me. – – V / V – – V / V – – V / V – ~ **(Hazaji musmali akhrabi makfufi maqsur)**

3. What is the name of a lyrical poem that expresses sadness in connection with the death of someone? – **Marcia**

4. This art refers to sequentially mentioning the names of several things or concepts in a verse, and then sequentially stating judgments about them. What kind of art are you talking about? – **Laff and nashr**

5. What is the meaning of the words Laff and

publication? - **Collection and dissemination**

6. What is the name of the art of referring to famous historical events, legends, literary works or proverbs in poetry or prose? - **Talmih**

7. What is the name of a poem with seven verses in each stanza? - **Musabba'**.

8. This evening, the moon is shining in my heart, It's not a gathering, the people of the sky are looking at each other with open eyes. (Note) Find the poetic art used in this stanza. - **husni talil**

9. What is the result of repetition of Mafailatun verse? - **Wafir**

10. Mustafilun, what is the result of repetition of activities? – **Mujtass**

11. It is an ornate couplet, and the poem has not one, but two rhymes. What kind of rhyme is it about? – **Zulqafiyatayn**

12. If all the words in two verses rhyme with each other, what type of rhyme is considered? - **tarsi'**

13. Life is hard for someone, and death is death for someone. What is the name of using opposite

words as a rhyme? - **Contrast rhyme**

14. What is the general name of the series of poetic forms widely used in Eastern classical poetry, which means "to string pearls on a string", "to arrange" in Arabic? - **Musamma**t

15. What is the name of a poem written in two languages in a certain order? -**Shiru-shakar**

16. What is the name of the shelter of the sea of Hazaj? - **muamm**o

17. I almost praised Jamal. What poetic art is used in this matla of Atoi's ghazal? – **musabba**

18. Which effect is formed from the repetition of foilotun, mustafilun? – Mujtass

19. What is the name of a rhyme that occurs in more than two rhyme styles, but the lines do not rhyme completely? - **Zulqavafi'**

20. What is the name of the smallest one-stanza poem in classical literature? – **Fard**

21. What is the rhyming type of rubai in the order a+a+a+a usually called? - **taronai ruboiy**

22. What is the name of the lyrical genre in a

solemn style that praises famous historical figures and great events? – **munsarih**

23. Who is the author of the philosophical ode "Tuhfatul Afkor" ("Gift of Thoughts")? - **A.Navoi**

24. Oppression is a disgrace to you, O watchful one. What poetic art is used in this stanza? –**tajnis**

25. What is the name of fa'lun (– –) of the root of foilotun? – **irsoli masal**

TICKET #19

1. Determine the weight of the following piece of cloth by Alisher Navoi.

   Wake up your two beautiful girls from their sweet sleep,
   Play in the flower garden until they fall asleep. – – V / V – – – / – – V / V – – – (**Khazaji musmali akhrab**)

2. Determine the weight of the following ghazali of Alisher Navoi.

   Soda sheikh forbids me to love you,
   Dema soda sheikh, I say loda sheikh. V–– – /V – – / V – – / V ~ (**Mutaqaribi musmali maqsur**)

3. What is the name of the fa' (–) zihof of the original Mafoiylun? – **Abtar**

4. What is the name of the muftailun (- VV -) of Mustafilun Asli? -**matviy**

5. What is the name of the root of foiloton (VV - ~)? - **mahbuni musabbag'**

6. What is the name of fa'lun (– –) zihof of the

original fauvlun? - **aslam**

7. Determine the weight of Ogahi's ghazal, which begins with "Mushkin's brow..." -   How dare Ogahi open his mouth and say a word,

the attack of a hundred sad deeds is difficult. – – V – / – – V – / – – V – / – – V – **rajazi musammani salim**

8. What is the name of the mafoiylu (V – – V) zihof of the original Mafoiylun? - **makfuf**

9. Which type of artistic art is based on proving a certain phenomenon not with real-life logic, but with poetic imagination-artistic logic? -**husni talil**

10. What is the name of a poem written in two languages in a certain order? -**Shiru**-**shakar**

11. What is the name of the shelter of the sea of Hazaj? – **makbuz**

12. It is a poem made up of stanzas, each volume equal to a ghazal and rhyming like a ghazal, in which the two verses at the end of each stanza have an independent melody. What lyrical genre are we talking about? – **Tarkibban**d

13. What is the result of the repetition of foilotun

and mustafilun? - **Khafif**

14. What is the name of a rhyme that occurs in more than two rhyme styles, but the lines do not rhyme completely? - **Zulqawafi'**

15. What is the name of the rhyming type of rubai in the order a+a+a+a, usually? - **taronai ruboiy**

16. What is the name of the lyrical genre in a ceremonial style that praises famous historical figures and great events? - **Qasid**a

17. Who is the author of the philosophical ode "Tuhfatul Afkor" ("Gift of Thoughts")? - **A. Navoi**

18. What is the name of the art of exaggerating and intensifying the state or action of an artistic symbol depicted in a literary work, which means "enlargement", "strengthening" in Arabic? – **Mubolag'a**

19. In which season were Amir Khusrav's "Oinai Iskandari" and Jami's "Khiradnomai Iskandari" written? – **Mutaqoribi musammani mahzuf** (V – –/ V – – / v – – / v –)

20. To which juzv does the form (VV –) belong? -

Fosilayi sugro

21. In which poetic art are elements such as means and basis found? - **tashbih**

22. Navoi's work "Sabbayi Sayyor" was created in which sea? - **Khafif**

23. Which word is formed from the repetition of foilotun, mustafilun? – **Khafif**

24. The general term for types of verses other than verses is... **musammat**

25. What is the name of the change of ramal bahr's failotun (VV - -)? – **Mahbun**

TICKET #20

1. Determine the weight of the following piece of cloth by Alisher Navoi.

   Look at my eyes, come and do science,

   make a country like a people under my eyes. V – V – / VV – – / V – V– / – – (**Mujtassi musamli mahbuni maqtu'**)

2. Analyze the verse of the following rubai of Babur.

   Sarrishtayi aishdin kungul zinhor,

   Uz oh, Zahiridin Muhammad Babur. **Hazaji musammani akhrabi maqbuzi salimi azall**

3. What is the name of Mustafilun asli's mafailun zihof? – **mahbun**

4. Who first used the term "poetics"? - **Aristotle**

5. What is the name of a poem written in two languages in a certain order? - **Shiru-shakar**

6. What is the name of the farm of Hazaj Bay? - **maqbuz**

7. Which of the poetic arts means "personalization" in Arabic? – **tashkh**

8. What is the result of the repetition of foilotun and mustafilun? – **Khafif**

9. What is the name of the lyrical genre in a solemn style that praises famous historical figures and great events? – **QASIDA**

10. What is the name of Babur's work dedicated to the science of aruz? - "**Mukhtasar**"

11. Which original column is not created from repetition? - **mafolot**u

12. In which book was the first ghazal written in Turkish? – **Ramal**

13. What is the name of the fo' (~) zihof of the original Mafoiylun? - **Azall**

14. Write down the 5th stanza of Ogahi's ghazal, which begins with "The jury of Mushkin Koshi...".

She is a flower-faced soul with the noise of the night and the morning.

Like a nightingale, she sings a hundred

and a thousand kinds of cries.

15. What is the name of failon (VV ~) of the root of foilotun? - **mahbuni mahzuf** 16. In which season was Navoi's work "Hayratu-l-abror" created? - **sari'**

17. Which of the "Khamsa" epics was created in Mutaqarib Bahr? - **"Saddi Iskandari**i"

18. I don't care about this trade. (Furqat) Find the poetic art used in this stanza. - **tazad**

19. What is the name of the art of referring to famous historical events, legends, literary works or proverbs in poetry or prose? - **Talmih**

20. What is the name of a poem with seven verses in each stanza? - **Musabba'**.

21. Mark the correct answer that the narrators in this verse indicate. I don't agree, a tear drops from my eye, I don't agree, my face turns a little pale. (H. Olimjon) - "z" sound in the **rhyming words "from my eyes - from my face"**. 22. Which bahr is formed from the repetition of Mutafailun Rukni? – komil.

23. What is the name of poetic art based on

homonymous words? – Tajnis

24. What is the name of Mustafilun (– –V ~) of the original Mustafilun? - **MUZOL**

25. What is the name of a poem with three lines per stanza? - You're welcome.

II. TEST QUESTIONS FROM THE SUBJECT "ARUZ AND CLASSICAL POETICS"

1. What is the paradigm of Ramali's mahzuf bahr?

A) V – – – \ V – – – \ V – – – \ V – –

B) – – V – \ – V – – \ – – V–\ – V –

C) – V– –\ – V – – \ – V – – \ – V – –

*D)– V – – \ – V – – \ – V– –\– V–

2. I have a lot of pain in your marriage, I have a lot of regrets. Find the meaning of the poem.

A) failotun mafo'iylun

B) mafo'iylun failotun

*C) failotun failatun

D) failotu failun

3. Take care of this world, O lover, One lover is a

master. Find the paradigm.

A) – V– \ – V – V \ V – –

* B)– – V \ V – V – \ V–~

C) V – – \ V – V – \ V – ~

D) – – V \ – B – B \ – B ~

4. There is a landscape equal to you in the wealth of undiscovered beauty,

Neither a landscape, a landscape witness, nor a witness, a witness is charming. (S. Saraoi) Determine the weight of the ghazal

. *A) hazaji musadami solim

B) hazaji musadami mahzoof

C) ramali musadami solim

D) ramali musaddasi mahzoof

5. If the verse consists of six columns, what term is it used for?

A) mustazad

B) *musaddas

C) murabba

D) m uzambal,

6. Which deviance is not characteristic of the network of mafoiylun rukni?

A) ashtar

B) abtar

C) azall

*D) mashkul

7. Which of the following is not characteristic of the network of the operating column?

A) mahbuni maqsur

*B) mahbuni muzol

C) maqtu'

D) mahbuni

8. In what weight did Husain Boykara create?

A) ramali musadasi salim

*B) ramaali musamali maqsur

C) ramali musadami mahzuf

D) ramali musaddasi maqzoof

9. What is the result of repetition of Mustafilun filotun columns?

A) Khafif

B) munsarih

*C) mujtass

D) Muzore'

10. I am happy with labor and suffering, I am familiar with pain wherever there is pain. Determine the size of the byte.

A) Rajazi musumali mahzuf

*B) Hazaji musumali mahzuf

C) Ramali musumali mahzuf

D) Hazaji musumali mahzuf

11. What was the weight of the first ghazal created in the Turkish language?

* A) Hazaji musaddali salim

B) ramali musaddali mahzoof

C) hazaji musaddasi maaksur

D) ramali musaddasi mahzoof

12. In what weight was the "Travel" of Muqimi written?

A) Ramali musaddasi mahzuf

* B) Rajazi murabbai salim

C) Ramali murabbai salim

D) Hazaji musaddasi salim

13. In what season is the genre of chicken written?

A) rajazi musaddasi mahzuf

* B) ramali musaddasi maksur

C) hazaji murabbai maksur

D) hazaji musaddasi mahzuf

14. Determine the weight of the ghazal "Karo ko'zum kelu mardumlig' emdi fan kilgil ..." by A. Navoi.

A) mutaqaribi maksuli mahzoof

B) muzarei maksuli makbuni makstui maksur

* C) mujtassi maksuli maksubi maktu'

D) munsarihi maksuli maktui maksoor

15. How much information about weight is given in Babur's work "Mukhtasar"?

A) 468

B) 511

C) 643 *

D) 537

16. Determine the paradigm of Ogahi's "Ustina" radiative ghazal.

A) – V – – \ –V— \ –V— \ –V—

B) V – – – \ V – – – \ V – – – \ V—

*C) – – V – \ – – V – \ – – V – \ – – V –

D) – V – – \ V – – – \ – V – – \ V – – –

17. What is the weight of Navoi's epic "Layli and Majnun"? *

A) hazaji musaddasi akhrabi maqbuzi mahzoof

B) ramali mussadi makfufi maqbozi mahzoof

C) mutaqaribi mussadi makfufi mahzoof

D) ramali musaddasi ashtari akhrabi mahzoof

18. In the ghurbat, the month of Hajri made me old,

   Hijran and the ghurbat affected me. Identify the drawing.

   A) —V–\ —V–\ —V–\ – V –

   B) – V –\ –V–\ –V–\ –V–

   *C) – – V \ V – – V \ V – – V \ V – –

   D) – V – \ V – – V \ – V – V \ –V–

19. Friends, don't party without me. (Munis). Find the weight.

   * A) ramali musmali mahzoof

   B) hazaji musmali ashtari akhrabi mahzoof

   C) rajazi musmali matviy

   D) hazaji musmali akhrabi makfufi akhtam

20. In what weight was Muqimi's comic book "Tanobchilar" written?

   A) hazaji murabbai mahzuf

   B) sari'i musaddasi matviyi makshuf

   C) muzorei musaddasi mahbuuni maqtu'

* D) rajazi murabbai salim

21. Fasli navbahor is dead, secretary winters, Friends, it is a prize, go for a walk, flowers. Define byte weight.

A) ramali musmali mahzuf

* B) hazaji musmali ashtar

C) khafifi musmali makfufi mahzuf

D) ramali musmali salim

22. Find the drawing of the verse "A stranger is not happy in a foreign land".

A) – – –\ V – – V \ V – V – \V –

B) – – V \ V – – V \ V – – V \ V –

*C) – – V \ V – V – \ V – – V \ V –

D) – – V \ V – – V \V – V – \V –

23. Leave it alone, traveler, if it's a planet, like me, you should take it, if it's poor, like me. Determine the weight.

* A) hazaji musmuli akhrab

B) rajazi musmuli matviy

C) rajazi musaddasi mahbuni maktu'

D) ramali musmuli mahbuni mahzoof

24. I love you, believe it or not,

I love you, believe it or not. Find the paradigm.

A) – – V – \ – – V – \– – V –

*B) —V\V—V\V—V\V—

C) –V– \—V–\–V– \—V–

Д) –V—\–V–\—V–\–V–

25. If they fly to other nations,

   they will find wisdom and go to the sky. (Hamza). Find the weight.

A) Hazaji Musamuli Solim

*B) Ramali Musamuli Mahzoof

C) Rajazi Musamuli Solim

D) Hazaji Musaddasi

26. In what weight was Muqimi's comic "Tanobchilar" written?

A) hazaji murabbai mahzuf

*B) sari'i musaddasi matviyi makshuf

C) muzorei musaddasi mahbuni maqtu'

D) rajazi murabbai salim

27. Friends, don't make a lady's song without me. (Munis). Find the paradigm.

A) – – V – \ – – V – \ – – V – \ – V –

B) V – – – \ V – – – \ V – – – \ V – –

C) – V – – \ V – – – \ – V – – \ V – – –

*D) – V – – \ – V – – \ – V – – \ – V –

28. In what weight was Navoi's epic "Farhad and Shirin" written?

* A) Hazaji musaddasi mahzuf

B) Ramali musadli mahbuni mahzuf

C) Rajazi musaddasi matvii

D) Ramali musaddasi mahzub

29. What is the weight of Rabghuzi's ghazal "Bahoriyot"?

A) hazaji musaddasi maqsoor

B) ramali musadami mahzoof

* C) hazaji musadomi salim

D) ramali musaddasi mahzoof

30. Bahalik dinar ul knowledge, It is priceless to ignorant without knowledge. Determine the efficiency.

A) Mafoilun mafoilun fauvlun

B) Failotun failotun failun

C) foilun foilun foilun foilun

* D) faulun faulun faulun foul

31. Leave it alone, traveler, if it's a planet, like me, and if you're a poor person, like me. Find the paradigm.

A) – – V – \ – – V – \– – V –

*B) —V\V—\—V\V—

C) –V– \—V–\–V– \—V–

D) –V—\–V–\—V–\–V–

32. In what weight was Zavqi's "Travel" written?

A) ramali musaddasi mahzuf

* B) rajazi murabbai salim

C) ramali murabbai salim

D) hazaji musaddai salim

33. In what weight was Navai's epic "Hayrat ul-Abror" created?

A) Munsarihi musaddasi mahbun

* B) Sariyi musaddasi matviyi makshuf

C) Hazaji musaddasi akhrabi mahzuf

D) Rajazi musaddasi matviy

34. Your letter is a tulip in a vegetable, Ul chashmi pur musumorin is a ghazal in a tulip. (Babur) Determine the weight.

A) rajazi musmami mavquf

B) mujtassi musmami mahbun

*C) muzorei musmami akhrab

D) khafifi musmami maqtu'

35. Find the paradigm of A. Navoi's ghazal "Karo ko'zum kelu mardumlig emdi fan kilgil ..."

A) V – V – \ – – V – \V – V – \ – –

B) V—V\V–V–\– V– V\—

C) V– – – \—V–\ –VV–\—

*D) V–V–\VV—\V–V–\—

36. What is formed by the repetition of the columns of Foiltun mustafilun?

A) muzore'

B) mujtass

C) munsarih

* D) khafif

37. Find the drawing of the verse "El anga shafiqu bolgash omish"

A) – – –\ V – – V \ V – V – \V –

B) – – V \ V – – V \ V – – V \ V–

*C) —V\V–V–\V– –V\V–

D) —V \ V – – V \V – V – \V–

38. You stayed this long, you did not die, Babur, excuse me, O Yorkie, blame me. Identify the drawing.

A) – – V – \ – – V – \ —V–\ – V –

B) – V – \ –V– \ –V– \ –V–

C) – V – \ V – – V \ – V – V \ –V–

*D) – – V \ V – – V \ V – – V \ V – –

39. Which deviation is characteristic of the network of interests?

A) beloved

B) dull

C) busy

* D) abtar

40. No one should be separated from the divine light like me, and the caring person should not be separated from the dildo. Find the weight.

* A) Ramali musmuli mahzuf

B) Hazaji musmuli mahzuf

C) Rajazi musmula muzol

D) Hazaji musmula salim

41. I pray for labor and suffering, I pray for you when there is pain. Define the paradigm.

A) – – V – \ – – V – \– – V –

B) —V\V—\—V\V—

*C) –V– \V—\–V– \V—

D) –V—\–V–\—V–\–V–

42. What is the name of the failun network of the Failotun column? *

A) mahbuni mahzuf

B) mahbuni sabbag'

C) mahbuni mahsur

D) busy

43. Fasli navbahor is dead, the secretary winters,

   Friends, it's a prize, go for a walk, Gulistans. Define the paradigm.

A) – – V – \ – – V – \– – V –

B) —V\V—\—V\V—

*C) –V– \V—\–V– \V—

D) –V—\–V–\—V–\–V–

44. What is the name of the muftailun network of the Mustafilun column?

A) mahbun

B) muzol *

C) matviy

D) mahbuni muzol

45. Yor kelur zamona does not exist, if he does not come - kelmasun netay, Sarf etara does not have a khazona, if he does not come - kelmasun netay. (Fun) Determine the weight of this byte.

* A) rajazi musmuli matviyi mahbun

B) ramali musmuli salim

C) hafifi musmuli musmuf

D) muzorei musmuli musmuf

46. Every time you hurt me, you cause a thousand pains. (Note) Define the paradigm.

A) – – V – \ – V – \ V – –

*B) — V \ V – V –\ V —

C) – V – – \ – V – \ – V –

D) – – V \ – V - V \ V - -

47. Friends, cry hard for my crazy state,

Who is alone, sometimes the grass falls on my heart. Determine the weight.

A) Khazaji musabbag

* B) ramali musakmul maqsur

C) rajazi musakmul muzol

D) hazaji musakmul mahzoof

48. What is the name of the foul network of Hazaj sea?

A) ajabb

B) azall

C) ashtar

D) akhtam

49. What bahr is formed from the repetition of Mafaoilatun verse?

* A) Wafir

B) Kamil

C) Munsarih

D) Mutadorik

50. When you come to open, show your identity,
Break the shackles and scatter everywhere. Find the weight.

A) ramali musmali mahzoof

B) khafifi musmali mahbun

* C) hazaji musmali ashtar

D) rajazi musmali matviy

51. Show the column that has nothing to do with Ruba'i weights.

A) abtar

B) maqbuz

*C) musabbagh

D) salim

52. Paradigm of Tuyuq genre?

A) – V – – \ V – – – \ – V – \ – V ~

B) V – – – \ V – – – \ V – – – ~

*C) – V – – \ – V – – \ – V ~

D) – V – – \ – V – – \ – V – – \ – V – ~

53. What is the result of repeating the columns of Mustafilun failotun?

A) Muzore'

*B) mujtass

C) munsarih

D) Khafif

54. I am the best Uvaisi to work and pains, I am the best Uvaisi when there is pain. Determine the size of the byte.

A) Hazaji custom

B) Ramali custom

C) Rajazi custom

D) Hazaji musamuli ashtar

55. What was the first ghazal paradigm created in Turkish?

* A) V – – – \ V – – – \ V – – – \ V – – –

B) – V – – \ V – – – \ – V – \ – V ~

C) V – – – \ V – – – \ V – – – ~

D) – V – – \ – V – – \ – V – – \ – V – ~

56. What is the paradigm of permanent "Travel"?

A) V – – – \ V – – – \ V – – –

B) – V – – \ – V ~

*C) – – V – \ – – V –

D) – V – – \ – V – – \ – V – – \ – V – ~

57 Who is the author of "Funun ul-baloga"?

A) Atullah Hosseini

* B) Ahmad Tarazi

C) Khalil ibn Ahmad

D) Furqat

58. There were surprisingly interesting conversations, Arz Etayn Emdi wrote down the names. Define byte weight.

A) hazaji murabbai mahzuf

*B) sari'i musaddasi matviyi makshuf

C) muzorei musaddasi mahbuni maqtu'

D) rajazi murabbai salim

59. What is the meaning formed by the repetition

of two identical and different columns?

A) Munsarih

* B) Sari'

C) Muzori'

D) Khafif

60. Determine the weight of the musaddad of Furqat "Sayding koya ber sayyad...".

* A) hazaji musmuli akhrab

B) rajazi musmuli matviy

C) rajazi musaddasi mahbuni maktu'

D) ramali musmuli mahbuni mahzoof

61. I love you, believe it or not, I love you, believe it or not. Find the paradigm.

A) – – V – \ – – V – \– – V –

*B) —V\V—V\V—V\V—

C) –V– \—V–\–V– \—V–

D) –V—\–V–\—V–\–V–

62. Which column does not benefit from the

exact repetition of one column?

A) Mafailatun

B) Mutafailun

* C) Maf'o'lotu

D) Failun

63. Which verse is formed by repeating the Mutafailun column?

A) Wafir

* B) Kamil

C) Munsarih

D) Mutadorik

64. In what weight was Muqimi's comic "Tanobchilar" written?

A) hazaji murabbai mahzuf

B) sari'i musaddasi matviyi makshuf

C) muzorei musaddasi mahbuuni maqtu'

* D) rajazi murabbai salim

65. Show the word that is not used in Uzbek

poetry.

A) Mutadoric

B) *Muqtazab

C) Sari'

D) Munsarih

66. In Uzbek poetry, indicate the part that is not used to form a verse.

A) The reason is beautiful, the fossils are sugro

B) The origin is beautiful, the reason is beautiful

* C) The fossils are beautiful, the reason is beautiful

D) The origin is beautiful, the fossils are beautiful

67. What is the Ashtar sea board of Hazaji?

A) V – – – \ – V – \ V – – –\ – V – *

B) –V–\V——\–V–\V——

C) –V– \—V–\ V— –\—V

– Д) –V—\–V–\—V–\–V–

68. May the pilgrimage of the month of Ghurbat make me old, Hijran and Ghurbat affect me. Identify the drawing.

A) – V –\ –V–\ –V–\ –V–

B) – V – \ V – – V \ – V – V \ –V–

*C) – – V \ V – – V \ V – – V \ V – –

D) —V–\ —V–\ —V–\ – V –

69. Friends, don't party without me. (Munis). Find the weight.

* A) ramali musmali mahzuf

B) hazaji musmali ashtari akhrabi mahzuf

C) rajazi musmali matviy

D) hazaji musmali akhrabi makfufi akhtam

70. He said: "Return, you madjnuni gumrah", He said: "Majnun vatadin rule agah". Find the byte weight.

A) Musaddasi of Ramali is incomplete

B) Musaddasi of Rajazi is muzol

*C) Musaddasi of Hazaji is incomplete

D) Musaddasi of Ramali is incomplete

II. A packet of questions for the final review.

1 Information about poetic weights.

2. Rukn, its structure and types.

3. Give information about the members.

4. Original columns.

5. Bahrs formed from the repetition of the same column.

6. List the mixed columns. Joint types.

7. Tell us about dream scientists.

8. A. Navoi - as a dream-reading scientist.

9. Words that are not used in Turkish poetry. Give information about toilets. Give examples of ghazals written in Ramali musmuli mahzuf bahr

11. There is only one landscape equal to you in the property of undiscovered happiness, Neither landscape, landscape witness, nor witness,

witness is charming. (S. Saraoi) Determine the weight of the ghazal.

12. Faulun column networks.

13. Foilun column networks.

14. Interest column networks.

15. Business column networks.

16. Mustafilun column networks.

17. Interest column networks

18. Babur is a scholar of dreams.

19. Tell us about the first ghazal written in Turkish. Mukimi's work "Travel" is about weight.

20. Information about the weight of the feathers.

21. Give information about the ruby genre weight.

22. The role of aruz weight in contemporary Uzbek poetry.

23. Muzori' sea networks. Light sea networks.

24. Networks of Mujtass Bahri. Networks of the Munsarih Sea. Networks of the Yellow Sea.

25. Weights of the work "Khamsa".

26. The weight of didactic epics.

27. Genres created in a strict weight.

28. The influence of Arabic aruzi on Persian-Tajik and Turkish poetry.

29. Akhrab family weights.

30. Ahram family weights.

31. Four column weights.

32. Six column weights.

33. Eight column weights.

34. Mutaqarib bahri weights. Mutadoric bhri weights.

35. Perfect sea weights. Hazaj Sea Weights. Ramal sea weights. Rajaz Bahri weights.

36. Published guides on the study of Aruz weight. Cause, homeland, fossil. Short, long and super long sentences.

37. Methods of determining the weight of Rubai. Bahrs, their structure and types. Two different columns.

38. Quantity changes. Quality changes. Both

quantity and quality changes. Weights of "Akhrabi Maqbuz" square. "Akhrabi Makfuf" shahabsha weights. "Akhrami ashtar" shahabsha weights. "Akhrami Akhrab" shahabsha weights. Aruz conquests. 39.The equivalent of sixteen columns is aslam weight.

40. The emergence of Aruz vaz in Turkish poetry.

41. Deep and deep seas. Aruz Circles.

42. Ways to identify bugs.

43. Methods of determining weights. Aruz sins. (azl, istihlof, imola, zihof, madd). Healthy. Dead weights. Furu'. Uzbek dream. About the term Aruz. Aruz during the Soviet era.

44. Wasl incident. Classic rhyme structure. Single rhyme. Murdaf (ridfli) rhyme. Muqayyad rhyme.

45. Institutional rhyme. Absolute rhymes. The weight of Mukimi's "Tanobchilar" comic. Taqte' (paradigm).

46. Aphayil and tafayl. Bahrs formed from Mafaiylun column. Bahrs formed from foilotun column. Bahrs formed from Mustafilun column.

47. Bahrs formed from the column of favors.

48. The weight of the work "Hayratul-Abror". "Farhad and Shirin" masnavi weight. The weight of the epic "Layli and Madnun".

49. The weight of the work "Sabai Sayor".

50. Weight of "Saddi Iskandari" masnavi.

51. May the Hajj of the month of Ghurbat make me old, Hijran and Ghurbat affect me.

52. Determine the weight of the gazelle.

53. The season has passed away, the secretary of the winters, Friends, it's a prize, go for a walk, flowers.

54. Determine the weight of the gazelle. Determine the weight of the following piece of furqat.

55. Leave it alone, traveler, it's like me if it's a planet, take your neck, it's poor like me.

56. Friends, don't party without me, don't make me sad when you drink. (Munis). Determine the weight of the gazelle.

57. A person with knowledge is worth a dinar, and an ignorant person is worthless without

knowledge. Determine the byte weight.

58. Your letter is a tulip in a vegetable garden, and your eyes are a ghazal in a tulip. (Babur) Determine the weight of the gazelle.

59. May no one be deprived of your divine light like me, may you not be deprived of your caring dildo.

60. Find the weight of the gazelle.

61. There is no time to come, if it doesn't come - it won't come,

62. There is no time to spend, if it doesn't come - it won't come. (Fun) Determine the weight of this byte.

63. When you come to open, show yourself, Break the shackles and scatter everywhere.

Milton Keynes UK
Ingram Content Group UK Ltd.
UKHW020331050824
446478UK00015B/523